Original title:
Wildwood Wonders

Copyright © 2025 Creative Arts Management OÜ
All rights reserved.

Author: Isaac Ravenscroft
ISBN HARDBACK: 978-1-80566-778-0
ISBN PAPERBACK: 978-1-80566-798-8

Light Over Lush Legacies

In the park where squirrels scheme,
Picnics attract ants like a dream.
A chipmunk wears a tiny hat,
Dancing round like a chubby cat.

Owl pretends to be aloof,
As a raccoon steals all the proof.
Bees buzz loudly, what a fuss!
While frogs join in with a chorus of 'hush!'

The Guardian's Echo

A tree stump holds a staff, you see,
An ancient sage, or just a bee?
His wisdom drips, a sticky tale,
Of how to eat and never fail.

Rabbits giggle under leaves,
While the fox trips on his own cleaves.
With a wink, the wise old tree,
Mumbles secrets, just for me.

The Woodland Philosopher

A snail debates a passing fly,
On matters deep, they both comply.
'Time is slow, or are we fast?'
They question life, but don't ask the past.

The pinecone jokes with the big old oak,
'Why did the twig cross the road to poke?'
'You've got me stumped, my leafy friend!'
They laugh so hard, they can't pretend.

Quest Among the Whispering Willows

Beneath the shade, a secret plot,
To find a treasure, or maybe not?
With laughter high and footsteps light,
They stumble on, through day and night.

A raccoon in a cloak so sly,
Claims he's a knight, oh my, oh my!
With each misstep, they all explode,
In fits of joy down the winding road.

Starlit Secrets of the Nightwood

Underneath the winking stars,
A raccoon aims for Mars.
He trips over a twig,
And dances like a jig.

An owl hoots a silly tune,
While fireflies shimmer like a moon.
A fox joins in with flair,
And whirls around with messy hair.

The trees sway with a grin,
As squirrels leap in a spin.
They laugh and jive with glee,
Underneath the towering tree.

A laugh is shared by all,
As shadows start to crawl.
The nightwood holds its charm,
Where giggles do no harm.

The Lure of the Woodland Stream

By the babbling brook so clear,
A turtle sings without fear.
He fumbles with his notes,
While fish swim and gloat.

A frog leaps in with flair,
Splashing water everywhere.
His croaks are quite the sound,
As laughter bounces 'round.

The dragonflies perform a show,
With moves that steal the flow.
They twirl and dip with grace,
Giving bugs a wild chase.

The stream hums with delight,
In the soft, fading light.
Nature's wise and quirky schemes,
Bring chuckles from our dreams.

Enchantment in the Timber

Deep within the forest's sway,
A raccoon plans a funny play.
He dons a hat too grand,
And takes his stance to stand.

Beneath the branches wide and tall,
A squirrel starts to sprawl.
He wiggles just like jelly,
And prances with a belly.

The shadows whisper jokes and cheer,
While woodpeckers lend an ear.
They tap with rhythm, feeling spry,
While the rabbits hop on by.

In this timber full of glee,
Laughter rings like a melody.
Even mushrooms seem to grin,
As the magic spins within.

Dance of the Wildflowers

In a field where blossoms sway,
A teddy bear leads the ballet.
With floppy ears and goofy grin,
He starts a twirl, spins and spins.

The daisies join with laughter bright,
While butterflies take flight.
A honeybee buzzes along,
Adding to the silly song.

The tulips sway their heads in jest,
As petals flutter like a fest.
A ladybug tries to keep the beat,
But tumbles down, quite a feat.

As the sun dips low, the dance goes on,
In the meadow, joy has grown.
A carnival of color and cheer,
Where even clouds stop to peer.

Reverie in the Leafy Sanctuary

In the shade, a squirrel prances,
Chasing dreams and short romances.
Leaves giggle as they sway in glee,
While bees hum tunes of jubilee.

A rabbit wears a tiny hat,
Dreaming up a dance with a cat.
They twirl beneath the dappled sun,
In this place, just having fun.

Mysteries of the Rooted Realm

Underneath the mossy floor,
A hedgehog plots with a quirky snore.
He claims to know the secret paths,
To hidden lands of giggles and laughs.

A wise old owl, with spectacles near,
Keeps a ledger of all who come here.
He spins tall tales with a wink and a grin,
Of mischievous gnomes and their silly sin.

The Enigma of the Wildwood

A raccoon in boots struts on the lane,
Stealing snacks like it's all in the game.
Trees dispute, they play their part,
In a hilarious play of heart.

A chattering chipmunk gathers his loot,
Announcing proudly, 'I'm quite astute!'
The ferns sway, they can't keep it in,
As laughter erupts from what's been drawn thin.

Silhouettes of Soaring Heights

Atop the hill, a crow caws loud,
Telling jokes to a passing cloud.
With each buoyant flap, he tells a tale,
Of squirrels on vacation, quite frail.

The sun dips low, the colors swirl,
While fireflies waltz and twirl,
In a dim-lit ball, with shadows tall,
Nature's jesters, amusing us all.

The Alchemy of Sunlight and Shade

In dappled light, the squirrels dance,
With acorns tossed, they take a chance.
A shadow slips, a branch does creak,
The sun plays tricks—who's hide and seek?

A bumblebee with style so bold,
Wears pollen like a crown of gold.
Slips on flowers, tables set,
A funny feast, don't place your bet!

Rhapsody of Rustling Leaves

The leaves make music, crisp and clear,
A rustle here, a whisper dear.
Dancing in circles, they laugh and sway,
Caught in a breeze, they twirl away!

A chipmunk rolls, what a sight to see!
With nuts in tow, so carefree.
He trips on roots and does a flip,
Wonders if he'll make the trip!

Tales from the Woodland Edge

A rabbit hops with nimble grace,
Chasing shadows all over the place.
A fox peeks out, with mischief bright,
Plans a game of tic-tac-tight!

A turtle yawns, "Oh, what a day!"
Moves so slow, he forgets the way.
In corners deep, he feels the sun,
And wonders why he ever runs!

The Spirit of the Clearings

In open spaces, chatter flows,
Where mushrooms dance and laughter grows.
A hedgehog spins, with spikes all round,
A prickly disco, what a sound!

A crow caws loud, with jokes to share,
Telling tales of the woodland affair.
With each riff and ruffle, they play it cool,
In the circus of trees, they rule the school!

Beneath the Gnarled Grasp

Beneath the trees with twisted limbs,
A squirrel's dance, it whims and skims.
He dropped his acorn, oh what a sight!
It bounced away, a true delight!

The owls all giggle, hoot in glee,
As raccoons play their tricks, carefree.
One steals a pie from a picnic late,
While the humans shout, 'Oh, what a fate!'

The Spirit of the Woodland Path

Down the path where shadows blend,
A fox and badger call 'Let's pretend!'
They wear a cloak made from leaves so fine,
And play tag with the sun, quite divine!

The rabbits laugh as they jump and dash,
While butterflies sprinkled like colorful ash.
But who's that lurking, so sly and fast?
A hedgehog with a wig and a squirrel's cast!

A Tapestry of Thorns and Blossoms

Among the thorns where daisies poke,
A porcupine made a straw hat joke.
He pricked a flower, watched it spin,
Then laughed so hard, he couldn't get in!

The bees buzz loud, but they won't stung,
They join the fun and begin to hum.
Wild roses blush at the comedic scene,
While ladybugs roll, 'We're living the dream!'

Illuminated by Starlit Canopies

Under the stars, with laughter ablaze,
A frog sings opera, a funny phase.
His croak quite grand, it echoes and rings,
The fireflies join in with their tiny blings!

A hedgehog waltzes with a dandy twist,
While mice in tuxedos dance, can't resist.
The moon chuckles down on this merry affair,
As woodland critters spin without a care!

The Language of Swaying Branches

In the breeze, the branches chat,
Telling tales of a bumbling cat.
Leaves do giggle, twigs do sway,
A squirrel's dance steals the display.

Acorns falling like clumsy jokes,
The trees all laugh, oh how they poke!
Rabbits hopping, tripping too,
Nature's laugh is shared by the crew.

Chronicles of the Woodland Whisper

Underneath the oak so grand,
A raccoon plays a one-man band.
Mice join in with tiny shakes,
While hedgehogs roll with silly quakes.

The whispers weave like clever threads,
As frogs croak tunes from their beds.
Barn owls hoot with perfect flair,
While fireflies twinkle without a care.

The Pulse of the Forest Floor

Down below, the pine cones snicker,
While mushrooms glow—a magic sticker.
Worms wiggle in their underground ball,
Nature's jesters, one and all.

A beetle rolls its prize so round,
While ants parade without a sound.
The pulse beats on with every bump,
In the earth's dance, they twist and jump.

Shadows of the Forgotten Glade

In the glade where shadows meet,
A dancing shadow taps its feet.
Ghostly laughs echo through the night,
While owls hoot in pure delight.

Mushrooms gossip on soft moss beds,
Of all the silly things they've said.
Branches wave like they've got style,
In the glade, fun stretches a mile.

The Gentle Heart of Nature

In a forest so lush and green,
The squirrels dance, the birds preen.
A rabbit hops with a skip and a twirl,
While a lazy bear watches, giving a whirl.

A deer trips over its own long legs,
Chasing a butterfly, with funny pegs.
The trees giggle as they bend and sway,
Nature's jesters putting on a play.

Incantations of the Underbrush

In shadows deep where brambles hug,
A hedgehog sighs, feeling snug.
With twigs for wands, the critters chant,
Casting spells for a dancing ant.

A gopher pops up with a dainty grin,
Declaring himself as the royal kin.
With acorns tossed like confetti in the air,
Each laugh reflects nature's flair.

The Lullaby of the Pines

Pines hum softly in the breeze,
While chipmunks plot their nutty schemes.
A raccoon moonwalks, oh what a sight,
Stealing snacks under the pale moonlight.

Squirrels hold a silent debate,
Over which branch makes the best plate.
With giggles echoing through the night,
Nature sings, what a funny delight!

Secrets of the Whispering Winds

The wind whispers tales of silly things,
Of frogs with crowns, and dragonfly wings.
A caterpillar jokes, 'I'll be a butterfly,'
While a wise old owl just rolls his eye.

A breeze tickles shrubs, making them giggle,
As the whole forest shares a little wiggle.
With secrets shared from the tall to the small,
Nature's laughter embraces us all.

Whimsy in the Woodland Breeze

A squirrel in a tiny hat,
Dances with a little rat.
They twirl among the leaves of green,
As if they're part of a grand routine.

The rabbits giggle, tails in air,
While frogs jump high without a care.
The trees join in with creaky sighs,
And whisper secrets to the sky.

A hedgehog rolls like a bowling ball,
Causing chaos, oh what a fall!
Mushrooms laugh with giddy glee,
"Join our party, come and see!"

So if you roam this energetic scene,
Keep an eye for the pranksters unseen.
In the woodland, where laughter rings,
Nature wears her silliest things.

The Solitude of Moss-Covered Stones

Beneath the shade of stones so round,
A turtle tells tales, joy abound.
"I'm faster than you think," he brags,
While dragonflies tie up their rags.

Mossy warts on the rocks proclaim,
"Who needs to be fancy or feel shame?"
A giggle rolls through the roots nearby,
As grasshoppers leap, oh me, oh my!

The quiet stones conspire and plot,
"How about we hold a cooking pot?"
But with no arms, they sulk and sigh,
While sneaky ants pass by with pie.

In solitude where mosses thrive,
They dream of parties, oh to be alive!
A stone's life may seem rather bleak,
Yet laughter blooms with every squeak.

Light Through a Whispering Canopy

The sunbeams shimmy through leaves up high,
As butterflies twirl like they can fly.
"Catch me if you can!" they tease the breeze,
While sneaky squirrels hide behind trees.

"Twinkle, twinkle," the fireflies hum,
With glow-in-the-dark dance moves—so fun!
Branches sway with a jovial grace,
As shadows play a merry chase.

The bees are buzzing a silly tune,
"Let's have a dance under the moon!"
A raccoon winks with mischief and cheer,
He knows the best snacks are always near.

In this canopy where laughter spins,
You may stumble upon woodland grins.
So follow the giggles, let joy be key,
In a place where nature's wild and free.

The Canvas of Nature's Palette

Swirls of color paint the ground,
With pink and yellow all around.
A beaver's hat crafted from fluff,
Says, "I'm stylish—ain't that enough?"

The daisies laugh with a splash of white,
While butterflies flaunt in pure delight.
"Who wore it best?" they chirp as they flit,
In every petal, there's a perfect fit!

Crickets hum in rhythm, it seems,
Creating a symphony of dreams.
And when the wind stirs a sea of grass,
Colors giggle, as if to pass.

This canvas spreads wide—wild and bright,
Where every corner bursts with light.
So dance with colors, hop and twirl,
In nature's art, let joy unfurl!

The Chronicle of Twisting Vines

In a jungle of twists, vines have their way,
They tangle my feet; oh what a display!
A raccoon in a hat claims he's the chief,
My laughter erupts amidst my disbelief.

Bouncing off branches, a squirrel goes rogue,
With acorn in paw, he starts quite the vogue.
Each twist of the vine brings a new funny pose,
As frogs with top hats strike silly disco throes.

Butterflies giggle at my comical plight,
As vines tie me up with such pure delight.
The world's upside down in this vine-laden spree,
Oh twist me again, won't you set me free?

Steps Amongst the Scatter

Footsteps echo where the wild things play,
A donut-shaped mushroom is here to stay.
Twirling in circles, the hedgehogs compete,
In this circus of chaos, life feels so sweet.

Scattered pine cones become little hats,
As badgers take selfies with fluffed-out spats.
Laughter erupts from the neighbors next door,
As raccoons debate who's the best at 'bore'.

Each step is a dance, each misstep a cheer,
With giggling grasshoppers offering beer.
Oh what a place where silliness reigns,
In steps of scatter, we banish the plains!

The Embrace of Autumn's Glory

Leaves chuckle softly as they start to fall,
They swirl like dancers, inviting us all.
With pumpkins in tow, I bounce with glee,
While squirrels throw acorns, aiming for me!

In flannels that squeak, we embrace this place,
The autumn air brings whimsy and grace.
Each corn maze adventure is filled with surprise,
As ghosts in the corn play peek-a-boo with our eyes.

The cider flows freely, sweet like a dream,
While laughter erupts like an unstoppable stream.
Oh autumn, you prankster, with colors so bright,
You tickle our senses, from morning to night!

The Sunlit Path of Secrets

Beneath the tall trees, where shadows convene,
A path of pure mischief, so quirky and keen.
Where whispers of squirrels plan a grand heist,
And giggles erupt from a hedgehog quite spiced.

The path reveals secrets in giggly bends,
A dance of the critters, where fun never ends.
With mushrooms that caper and flowers that grin,
This sunlit pathway wears a cheeky skin.

A trail full of laughter, a jumble of cheer,
With gnomes holding signs that say, "Join us, dear!"
So come take a stroll and you might just see,
The sunlit path's laughter is waiting for thee.

Backwoods Ballad

In a clearing, a squirrel danced,
Twisting and twirling, oh how he pranced!
He tripped on a log, then fell with a thud,
Sprayed mud on a frog who was sleeping in mud.

A raccoon joined in, with a hat made of leaves,
Claiming he's royalty, if only he believes.
A chipmunk declared, 'I'm the king of this beat!'
But tumbled right over, tripped up on his feet.

They held a big feast of acorns and grass,
With laughter a-plenty, as time seemed to pass.
The moon brought a glow, and they took to the sky,
Chasing after fireflies, oh my, oh my!

At dawn, they all settled, tired and content,
Swapping tall tales of the night that they spent.
In the backwoods, such fun, oh, what a delight,
Who knew that mischief could feel so just right!

Feast of Fragrant Blossoms

The bees hosted parties where nectar's the treat,
With tiny invites tucked in every sweet seat.
A butterfly swooped, showing off all her flair,
Then tripped on a petal—what a sight in the air!

A badger brought cakes made of mud and some grass,
Claiming they're gluten-free—'Come, try if you pass!'
But a hedgehog nearby said, 'That's quite a joke,
You need more than foliage for food, you old bloke!'

They chortled and giggled while munching on blooms,
As the daisies chatted, and the lupines hummed tunes.
In this fragrant fest, laughter filled up the day,
Who knew wild flowers could serve such a bouquet?

So if you should wander where blossoms abound,
Look for the critters who dance on the ground.
Join in on the fun, let your worries dissolve,
Where laughter and nature happily evolve!

Passage Through the Elm

Beneath the old elm, a story unfolds,
With giggles and whispers, the secret it holds.
A raccoon on a branch thought he'd give it a try,
But slipped on a leaf, and oh, how he did fly!

The squirrels all chuckled, hanging upside down,
As he landed in moss, with a thump and a frown.
'Next time,' he proclaimed, with a wink and a grin,
'I'll stick to the ground and let the acorns win!'

A wise old owl gave advice from the tree,
'Life's just a ride, filled with humor, you see?
So laugh off your tumbles, embrace all the fun,
And who knows, my friend, you might just be the one!'

As daylight faded, tales danced on the wind,
The elm stood proud, where mischief begins.
And all through the night, creatures laughed without fear,
For joy in the forest is always near!

Storylines of the Sprawling Branches

Up high in the branches, a narrative thrived,
With characters soaring, like dreams that arrived.
A catbird was crooning, completely off-key,
While a raccoon nearby laughed, 'Hey, that's not me!'

The branches held tales of old antics and charms,
Where a possum played dead, and nobody warms.
In the midst of the laughter, a bumblebee buzzed,
Saying, 'Life is absurd, you've got to just fuzz!'

As the sun dipped low, they gathered to share,
All the stories of folly that danced in the air.
With snacks made of berries and a dash of delight,
The critters all knew they were set for the night.

So if you seek tales where the laughter grows loud,
And nature's the stage, with a jovial crowd,
Just follow those branches, let the stories unfurl,
For there's magic in giggles that shimmer and twirl!

Veils of Moss and Magic

In the forest deep, where shadows play,
Mossy hats on squirrels, they dance all day.
Rabbits in coats, each with a flair,
Bouncing with giggles, without a care.

A snail in a race, oh what a sight,
Cheering from trees, what a delight!
Owls hoot in laughter, it's quite a scene,
Chasing a beetle, oh so keen!

A hedgehog shifts, dressed in style,
Wearing a grin that goes a mile.
Frogs leap in harmony, croaking a tune,
Under the glow of the silver moon.

The winds whisper secrets, tickling the leaves,
Telling the tales of the playful eves.
Nonsense abounds in this leafy domain,
A wild and whimsical, joyful refrain.

The Glimmering Leaf Trail

On a path of glimmer, where laughter trails,
Dancing with fireflies, we set our sails.
A fox in a bowtie, oh what a sight,
Sipping on dew while sipping moonlight!

The acorns debate, who's roundest of all,
While chipmunks giggle, and squirrels enthrall.
Through giggles and snorts, oh what a chuckle,
As shadows of giggles make every heart buckle.

The wise old toad sits, caffeine afire,
Sharing his secrets, our hearts he'll inspire.
In this magical maze, not one dull face,
Laughter erupts, it's a cozy embrace!

Pinecones are bouncing, like fuzzy balls,
Filling the air with their playful calls.
Branches are tickling, everyone's free,
In this glimmering trail, just you and me!

Shadows of Ancient Trees

Beneath twisted branches, giants they stand,
Tickling the sun with their leafy hand.
A raccoon in pajamas steals all the snacks,
While woodpeckers drum on the old knotted backs.

In the canopy's depths, the squirrels convene,
Plotting their mischief, so clever and mean.
The air is a buzz with chatter and fun,
While shadows of laughter dance in the sun.

A turtle named Tim wears a party hat,
Swaying to tunes of a whimsical brat.
Near streams bubbling joyfully, frogs all croon,
Holding a rave by the light of the moon.

Each rustle and whisper a playful jest,
In this ancient realm, we're truly blessed.
The trees watch above, sharing funny lore,
Filling our hearts as we laugh by the shore.

The Atlas of Burgeoning Life

In the atlas of giggles, where all dreams collide,
Flowers in bowties swell with pride.
Worms have a dance, wriggling in rows,
Twirling with glee, where the funny tree grows.

Butterflies gossip, swirls in a trance,
Painting the sky in a colorful dance.
With each fluttering laugh, the petals unleash,
A symphony colorful, a wonderful feast.

The bees hold a conference regarding their buzz,
While ants in formation keep moving with fuzz.
Each creature a page on this whimsical map,
Mapping their antics in laughter's warm lap.

Every rustle tells tales of mischievous glee,
Nature's own jesters, wild and so free.
Here in this haven, where life blooms so bright,
The atlas unfolds, day turns into night.

Twilight Dreams Among the Pines

In the quiet shadows, critters prance,
Squirrels doing silly little dance.
Owls hoot jokes from boughs so high,
While the stars wink down, a cosmic pie.

Bats swoop in for evening snacks,
Chasing moths along the tracks.
Moonlight spills like lemonade,
Nature's twist on a playful charade.

Willy-nilly gusts of breeze,
Scatter giggles among the trees.
Each bird's tune a merry trick,
Making night seem oh-so-quick!

As dreams unfold in piney embrace,
Everyone's wearing a silly face.
A rabbit's wiggle, a fox's spin,
In the twilight, let laughter begin!

The Mystique of Moss-Covered Stones

Mossy rocks in a verdant cloak,
Whisper secrets that make me choke.
Giggles of fairies dance on the breeze,
Telling tales of ancient trees.

Each stone grins with a greenish frown,
Winking at squirrels racing down.
A snail's slow salute, a toad's big laugh,
While critters share a weathered craft.

'Why so serious?' a tiny frog croaks,
As lichen clings like wise old folks.
Every rock a joke, every shade a pun,
In this quirky realm, we all have fun!

So come along and find your groove,
Among these stones, let laughter move.
In mossy majesty, life's a play,
Where humor enchants and brightens the day!

Ferns and Fireflies at Dusk

Ferns wave hello in the twilight air,
While fireflies twinkle without a care.
They flash their bulbs, a disco surprise,
Leading the way for moonlit spies.

In shadows thick, a raccoon grins,
Stealing snacks while the night begins.
With a rustle and giggle, he moves so sly,
Twirling and swaying beneath the sky.

Fireflies are jesters with bright little lights,
Painting the air with their dazzling flights.
"Catch me if you can!" they seem to tease,
While frogs join in with their ribbiting pleas.

"Oh, what a party!" the crickets cheer,
As laughter and light fill the atmosphere.
Nature's own joke in a magical dusk,
With ferns and fireflies, come join the fun!

Guardians of the Ancient Trees

Tall trees loom like ancient guards,
Cracking jokes in leafy yards.
Their roots are tangled, quite the sight,
While squirrels scurry in morning light.

With bark like wrinkles full of lore,
They gossip of times we can't ignore.
"Remember that storm?" a spruce chimes in,
"Should have seen the mischief back then!"

Their branches sway to a rustling tune,
With bears attempting a dance 'neath the moon.
Each whispering leaf, a giggly quirk,
While owls chuckle at nature's work.

So skip and jump under their shade,
Join in the fun; don't be afraid!
In the presence of giants, laughter's the key,
For ancient trees hold the joy of the spree!

Colors of the Forest Dawn

In the morning light, the trees wear green,
A jaunty hat just like a scene.
Squirrels twirl in acorn hats,
While dancing leaves invite the bats.

Sunbeams crackle through the leaves,
The laughter of the wood, it weaves.
A raccoon makes a grand debut,
He lost a shoe; now what to do?

Mushrooms giggle in shades so bright,
As butterflies take off in flight.
In every nook, a creature plays,
Painting mornings in silly ways.

A chubby badger starts to croon,
In a top hat that shines like the moon.
The forest is a lively dream,
Where even logs can giggle and gleam.

Beneath the Canopy of Dreams

Underneath the leafy roof,
A mouse sings ballads far aloof.
A chorus of frogs joins the fun,
Their croaks a tune, oh what a run!

A busy bee forgot her flight,
Tangled in a spider's kite.
She buzzes loud, with mighty zest,
While spiders giggle, 'Is that a fest?'

A fox in glasses reads a book,
His friend the owl gives a puzzled look.
Words get twisted, so silly, so bright,
In a forest where dreams take flight.

Giggling squirrels play peek-a-boo,
With acorns dropping by the crew.
In this place where whimsy reigns,
Every heart knows joy and gains.

The Language of Ferns

Ferns whisper secrets, oh so sly,
To beetles who attend the spy.
In their fronds, they write a jest,
'What's green and awkward? Oh, that pest!'

They talk of snacks and leafy dreams,
Of bugs dressed up in fancy themes.
A ladybug is queen today,
In a crown made of dirt and hay.

The wise old trunks roll their eyes,
At gossip flitting in the skies.
'What do you think?' a lizard beams,
'More stories from the ferny schemes?'

And thus they chatter, all aglow,
In a world just for giggles to flow.
With every leaf, a twist and turn,
In the dance of life, the ferns all learn!

Fables of the Fern Gully

In the gully, tales unfold,
Of brave young critters, bold and gold.
A tortoise with a top hat, smart,
Saves the day with a clever art.

Mice wear capes and zoom around,
Playing heroes, so astound!
While fireflies host a grand ball,
Each flickering whimsy does enthrall.

There's a gossiping brook that flows,
Telling stories as it goes.
'Did you see Mr. Chipmunk dive?
He cannonballed, oh how he thrived!'

As night falls, the stars all cheer,
For every silly tale brought near.
In the fables where laughter sways,
The gully dreams and frolics praise.

A Tapestry of Twigs and Tales

In the thicket, a squirrel grins,
Hoarding acorns, collecting wins.
A bird in a hat sings a rhyme,
Complaining about the weather's crime.

A hedgehog rolls by, looking chic,
In a coat made of leaves, antique.
While rabbits play cards under a tree,
Betting on carrots, quite the spree!

An owl laughs loud, on his nightly rounds,
Telling tall tales of far-off towns.
The trees sway gently, clapping applause,
For the jesters of nature, with their faux pas.

The night ends with a wink and a grin,
As the forest's parties begin again.
With twigs and tales woven tight,
The wildwood giggles into the night.

The Heart of the Humble Grove

In the heart of the grove, giggles abound,
Where mushrooms wear shoes upon the ground.
A shy little mouse throws a dance,
While crickets engage in a sing-along chance.

A raccoon with a bandana so bright,
Swipes snacks from the ants, just for delight.
A turtle in shades moves slow but sly,
Charming the flowers, oh my, oh my!

The owls debate in a very loud hush,
Over who looks best in shades of bush.
The bees wear tiny crowns, floating free,
In the heart of the grove, all's a jubilee.

As twilight whispers, the laughter keeps,
With dreams of nuts, while the forest sleeps.
Nature's jesters, one and all,
In the humble grove, where wild joys call.

The Dance of the Silver Stream

Down by the stream, in a tippy-toe dance,
Fish wear bow ties, giving romance a chance.
Frogs leap in sync with a splash and a croak,
While turtles all chuckle at the joke!

A raccoon on the bank, juggling stones,
In a comical contest with his silly bones.
The ducks quack out tunes, a band of their own,
While the dragonflies twirl, in a glittering zone.

The moonbeam winks at the bubbly jest,
As critters all gather for nature's best fest.
With laughter a-plenty from dawn until dusk,
In the dance of the stream, there's joy to trust.

As ripples giggle and shimmer with cheer,
The world grows brighter with each passing year.
In waters where laughter sings like a dream,
Life flows funnily in the silver stream.

The Woven Wisdom of the Trees

Among the trees, wise whispers flow,
Each branch a sage, with tales to bestow.
The oak grins wide, sharing old lore,
While pine needles weave stories galore.

A squirrel took notes, with a pencil so small,
Wondering how trees can outsmart them all.
A woodpecker's knock forms a beat that's divine,
As they hold a debate over dinner and wine.

Each leaf flutters gently, nodding in glee,
Agreeing that laughter's the best cup of tea.
With roots that dig deep, wise words are bestowed,
In the woven embrace of the tree's leafy road.

As day turns to night, stories take flight,
In the grand tapestry, woven bold and bright.
Laughter and wisdom, they twine and they seize,
In the woven wisdom of the humbling trees.

Foliage of Forgotten Dreams

In the woods where squirrels play,
They gather snacks throughout the day.
A raccoon sneaks in, oh what a sight,
Dancing with shadows, oh what a fright!

Leaves whisper secrets, green then gold,
Tales of mischief, daring and bold.
A fox trips over his own furry feet,
Chasing a butterfly, oh what a treat!

Mushrooms giggle beneath the trees,
As squirrels conspire with the buzzing bees.
They put on a show, the woodland's delight,
A circus of antics, pure silly might!

Beneath the boughs, where laughter rings,
Nature plots all the funniest things.
With twinkling eyes and a playful breeze,
Every moment here is sure to please.

The Tranquil Embrace of Nature

Bees wear tiny hats, with style quite sweet,
While daisies nod heads in rhythmic beat.
A turtle in sunglasses, moves so slow,
He's on a wild stroll, in leisure's flow.

A chorus of frogs, croak 'til they're hoarse,
Join in the fun with nature's own force.
The brook gurgles jokes only fish get,
While the cool breeze sways with no regret.

Pine trees stand tall, wearing clouds like caps,
While chipmunks play hide and seek with naps.
A breeze tickles leaves, inviting a grin,
As raccoons plot mischief, let the fun begin!

With each rustle and tumble, laughter ignites,
In this serene realm, where joy takes flights.
Nature's embrace, a whimsical show,
Creating moments where silliness flows.

The Quest through Mossy Footprints

Down a path where stories grow,
Footprints muddy, on the go!
A hedgehog peeks from a leafy nook,
Critiquing the pages of every book!

Mossy slippers tell the tale,
Of creatures gone with a giggly wail.
A raccoon plays detective with style,
While the owls hoot softly, wearing a smile.

Pitter-patter of paws on the ground,
A bunny hops by, with giggles abound.
They map the knolls with whimsical grace,
With shadows dancing in every place.

Chasing a squirrel, this journey's twist,
A treasure of laughter cannot be missed.
With each pounce and skip, they share their delight,
The quest of the forest, a comical sight!

The Palette of the Season's Change

When the trees turn from green to red,
A parrot complains, 'Where's my comfy bed?'
Pumpkin patch parties, oh what a scene,
With scarecrows dancing in denim and green!

The winds of autumn swoosh and sway,
While squirrels are busy, what a display!
Painting their acorns with giggles galore,
Leaving fuzzy feathers on nature's floor.

A hedgehog in stripes, how quirky and fun,
Thinks he's a tiger, oh, what a pun!
The whispers of leaves, a ticklish tune,
As critters plan dances beneath the moon.

With every brushstroke, nature's delight,
Colors collide in a joyful flight.
From sunrise to sunset, laughter takes stage,
In the theater of seasons, we're all the rage!

The Heartbeat of the Thicket

In the thicket where squirrels play,
Every acorn's a treasure, they say.
Trees whisper secrets, leaves dance in glee,
Even the bushes once dreamed to be free.

The fox wears glasses, quite sharp and astute,
While rabbits debate, wearing tiny suits.
Frogs throw a party, with flies as the snack,
Life in the thicket is never off track.

Skunks hold conventions, all hoping to smell,
They argue 'bout perfume, they argue quite well.
A bear breaks the rules, trying to get slim,
His diet of donuts is sinking him grim.

But laughter's the anthem, they chuckle with cheer,
In this world of whims, there's nothing to fear.
Join in the fun, hear the giggles evolve,
For among all this chaos, we all can resolve.

Oath of the Ancient Ones

The mighty oaks gather, tall and grand,
Swearing their vows, as tall trees take stand.
Whispers of wisdom flow through their roots,
While the beetles debate in their leafy suits.

Caterpillars promise to dance on the breeze,
Moths peek from the shadows, enticed by the tease.
The wise old owl hoots, 'Jokes are our game!'
With a wink and a nudge, they're not all the same.

Vows of mischief wrapped in purple vines,
The raccoons' antics draw laughter in lines.
Climbing the branches, they giggle and roll,
Nature's jesters, it's life without toll.

Amidst all the whispers, the giggles collide,
The ancient ones laugh, with joy as their guide.
In this realm where the curious roam,
The trees stand their watch, calling all to come home.

Glimpse of the Mystic Pathway

Down a pathway of shadows kissed by light,
Gnomes play cards with a flicker of fright.
The mushrooms all giggle, quite proud of their shade,
As the pathway reveals secrets never displayed.

Bunnies dressed up for a bash in the glen,
Dancing on daisies with rhythm and zen.
They twirl in the moonlight, tails wobbling free,
While a hedgehog DJ spins tunes of pure glee.

The glow-worms flicker, like stars on the ground,
Leading lost wanderers back to the sound.
A raccoon in disguise tells tales of the land,
With a clipboard in paw, he's got dreams so grand.

In this whimsical realm, let laughter unite,
With each step we take, there's wonder in sight.
For magic's a journey we're all meant to take,
On pathways that shimmer, where friendships awake.

The Guardian of the Glade

In the heart of the glade, a brave guardian stands,
A hedgehog in armor, with well-guarded plans.
He guards all the critters, from squirrel to snail,
With stories of courage he'd eagerly hail.

His shield made of leaves, his sword from a stick,
He battles the wind with a confident flick.
The crickets all cheer, tapping feet in the dirt,
While fireflies join in, without a moment's hurt.

The wisps came to dance in the soft evening glow,
Twisting and twirling, as breezes would blow.
The guardian chuckles, feeling quite grand,
His kingdom is lively, it's better than planned.

With giggles and joy, they keep watch through the night,
In this realm of delight, where all feels so right.
So raise up a glass—made from acorn, of course—
To the guardian of laughter, our nature's true force!

Tides of the Woodland Seasons

In spring, the leaves do flutter,
As squirrels chase each other in a mutter.
Frogs sing a chorus, quite off-key,
While ants march home with bits of brie.

Summer sun warms the mossy space,
A raccoon races, wearing a face.
Bunnies hop with such great flair,
While deer stop by for a good old stare.

Autumn leaves swirl in a dance,
Chipmunks nibble with a glance.
Mushrooms pop like little hats,
While hedgehogs roll like acrobats.

In winter's chill, the branches creak,
Snowmen stand where fairies peek.
The forest holds its breath so tight,
As snowflakes fall in soft moonlight.

The Forgotten Realm of Thicket Dreams

In thickets dense, the rabbits plot,
To steal the carrots—oh, what a lot!
A fox in socks, with such a grin,
Plots out a picnic, hoping to win.

The owls take bets on who will trip,
As mushrooms dance and brew a sip.
The crickets chirp their evening song,
While fireflies buzz, it won't be long.

On nights so bright, the raccoons play,
Among the leaves, they sip and sway.
A hedgehog dreams of acorn stew,
While squirrels trade a treasure or two.

And when the morning sun does rise,
All creatures dress in funny ties.
A world of whimsy, not too far,
In thicket dreams, we find bizarre.

Whispers of the Untamed Grove

In the grove, whispers float like air,
Where squirrels make quite the cheeky pair.
Birds share gossip with giggles loud,
And trees wear crowns, oh-so-proud.

Mice scurry in a huddle, keen,
Sipping dew like it's a scene.
In shadows, shadows play peek-a-boo,
While hedgehogs joke in playful view.

A bear in boots gives a charming twirl,
As butterflies race in a silly whirl.
The crunch of leaves is a rhythm sweet,
Where even the grumpy badger finds a beat.

When night falls, the stars come out,
The moonlight dances, without a doubt.
In nature's lair, laughter's the key,
Whispers of joy, wild and free.

Enchanted Canopy

Beneath a canopy woven tight,
Giggles echo, oh, what a sight!
The parakeets throw a lively bash,
While critters join in, a color splash.

The owls wear glasses, pretending to read,
As tree trunks dance to a funky creed.
Bunnies juggle berries just for fun,
While beavers shoot hoops, 'til the day is done.

A turtle in shades dines on pie,
While branches sway and whirl on high.
The wind tells stories, but in disguise,
Echoes of laughter fill the skies.

At twilight's edge, the fun takes flight,
Creatures twirl in the soft twilight.
Under the stars, they all convene,
In the enchanted grove, ever green.

Enchanted Shadows of the Glade

A squirrel stole my sandwich today,
He danced on the branch, all carefree and gay.
I shouted, "Hey, that's a very bold move!"
But he just winked, said, "I've got the groove!"

The fox in the corner starts to take bets,
On who'll get my crumbs—my dinner regrets.
A raccoon rolls up with a sly little grin,
"Mind sharing some pie? I just love whipped thin!"

The owls hoot loudly, they're wasting no time,
Making their plans over muffins and thyme.
The shadows are laughing, carrying cheer,
In this glade full of laughter, no worries, no fear!

A rabbit hops by, with a wink and a hop,
"Why worry about crumbs? Just join in the slop!"
As the night settles in, and the stars start to shine,
The glade sings a song that's perfectly fine.

The Song of Leaf and Root

Once I met a beetle, quite dressed in flair,
He challenged a snail for a race in the air.
"Let's see who's the fastest, I'm ready to zoom!"
The snail just looked up, "I'll wait in my room."

A leaf in the breeze said, "Why take it so slow?
Let's dance through the shadows, let spontaneity flow!"
The beetle took off, but forgot he could fly,
Hit a branch, did a flip—oh my, oh my!

A family of mushrooms sprang up with delight,
They chuckled and shimmered in soft, golden light.
"The faster you try, the more ground you can lose,
Just wiggle and jiggle, you silly little muse!"

The lesson was clear, as the sun started to fade,
In the song of the leaves, there's no rush to invade.
So let's leap and let laugh, in our own little way,
Tomorrow will come, and we'll dance in the day!

Murmurs from the Hidden Hollow

Down in the hollow, where secrets reside,
A chatty old owl took us all for a ride.
He said, "Gather 'round, let the gossip commence,
Have you heard about Bertie? He's leapin' the fence!"

The frogs croaked in laughter, they ribbited loud,
"Bertie's a legend, he's made us all proud!
Last week he tried flying, but just hit a tree,
Now he claims that he's better, just look at me!"

A tortoise, so slow, chimed in with a grin,
"Let the birds do the jumping, I'll just take my win.
With patience and wisdom, I'm destined to thrive,
And the tales of my wandering will keep me alive!"

So the critters all chuckled, sharing bits of their tales,
In the hidden hollow, amidst giggles and gales.
For laughter is magic, a joy to behold,
In the heart of the woods, where the stories are told.

Heartbeat of the Timbered Realm

In the timbered realm, where the sun breaks the night,
A weasel named Wilbur had quite the delight.
He juggled some acorns while riding a log,
"Watch me outshine that old grumpy frog!"

The frogs started ribbiting, "Oh, what a show!
But will you still juggle when we shout out 'go'?"
Wilbur just winked, said, "I'm ready to play!
But don't mind my flails if I drop one today!"

The trees held their breath, the audience gasped,
As acorns flew high, but he fumbled and clasped.
They tumbled and rolled, scattering like dreams,
And the laugh echoed wildly, or so it seemed.

With laughter as currency, this realm so divine,
Every critter a friend, oh, how their eyes shine!
So dance through the timber, let giggles be found,
In the heartbeat of laughter, the joy does resound.

Echoes Beneath the Bark

In the forest, squirrels plot,
Nuts are treasures, not forgot.
They giggle at the owls that hoot,
While foxes dance in raccoon boots.

The trees whisper silly tales,
Of cheeky deer on tiny trails.
The crickets chirp a funny tune,
As shadows waltz beneath the moon.

A hedgehog wears a spiky crown,
While rabbits bounce in jester's gown.
The mushrooms giggle, swaying near,
Adding humor to the woods' cheer.

In this realm of leafy fun,
Every creature's race is won.
Laughter echoes through bark's grace,
Nature's comedy takes its place.

Sylvan Secrets

In the thicket, secrets grin,
Where gnomes and frogs run off to spin.
Beneath the pines, a rabbit jests,
Claiming that he knows the quests.

The lazy bear hums a tune,
While bees compete to catch the moon.
A wise old owl with glasses cracked,
Shares stories of all that he lacked.

Chubby chipmunks play charades,
Not one of them gets the charades.
A fox peeks out, wearing a hat,
"Oh, where's my whiskers?" he says, "Rat!"

In this wood of funny sights,
Where mischief brews and joy ignites.
Every rustle, a giggle close,
In the glade where laughter flows.

The Dance of Foliage

The leaves shimmy with delight,
As squirrels host a wild dance night.
Each twig bends to the rhythm's call,
While shadows slip and softly fall.

In a circle, mushrooms prance,
While flowers sway in their romance.
A hedgehog twirled, forgot his spine,
Now rolls about, oh, so divine!

The wind plays tricks, a whispery tease,
As branches sway with utmost ease.
The sunbeams wink, the critters cheer,
Nature's ball, the fun is near!

Underneath the leafy dome,
Every creature feels at home.
With giggles and swirls, the wood does sing,
A joyous dance, a wild spring fling!

Hidden Glades of Mystery

In the glades where laughter hides,
The whispering ferns play silly slides.
A raccoon dons a rubber nose,
And tickles owls beneath their toes.

A fox with spectacles so grand,
Reads stories from a fairy band.
With every page, the trees all sway,
As if to join in on the play.

The brook bubbles with cheeky jokes,
While turtles groan at funny folks.
Behind the bushes, laughter grows,
With secrets that the forest knows.

In these glades, where mirth abounds,
Funny tales spin round and round.
Every rustle, a gift to share,
A tickling breeze, a joyful air.

The Symphony of Shrubbery

In the thicket, branches dance,
Squirrels hold a wild romance.
Birds attempt to sing in tune,
Frogs croak with a lumpy croon.

Leaves rustle with a playful cheer,
Rabbits hop, but disappear.
A raccoon steals my sandwich prize,
As I watch with wide-open eyes.

The bushes giggle, full of jokes,
While hedgehogs play with the folks.
A caterpillar starts a band,
With ants as backup, quite unplanned.

What a sight, this leafy crowd,
Nature's antics, vibrant and loud.
In the symphony of green delight,
Laughter echoes, day turns night.

Embrace of the Evergreen

Tall pines twist in silly ways,
Catching squirrels in a daze.
Boughs bend down with secret charms,
Hugging bees and buzzing farms.

Mossy carpets, soft and bright,
Slipping sloths in funny flight.
A woodpecker dons a cap,
Tapping rhythms in a nap.

A raccoon plays peek-a-boo,
While chipmunks cheer him on, woohoo!
Branches shake with secret jokes,
As laughter stirs the shady oaks.

Deep in the woods, we find our glee,
In every trunk, a mystery.
Each evergreen a funny friend,
Where giggles sprout and never end.

Traces of Forgotten Trails

Along the path, there's a gnome,
Claiming it's his leafy home.
Lost hikers meet a sign that reads,
'Watch for bears who steal your seeds!'

Twisty roots with jester hats,
Play tag with curious cats.
A bamboo maze leads nowhere fast,
While snails take bets on who'll come last.

Footprints speak of antics shared,
Of wandering folk who never dared.
Whispers echo through the trees,
As laughter floats upon the breeze.

In this realm where jokes remain,
Each step a tickle, a silly gain.
Find the paths both old and quirky,
Laughter's the prize—so never murky!

Fantasy in the Foliage

In the thicket, fairies hide,
Giggling while they sneak and glide.
With toadstool hats and slippers rare,
Chasing butterflies without a care.

A wizard's hat upon a branch,
Grows a gnome who loves to dance.
His crooked moves, a sight to see,
As leaves applaud with glee and glee.

Treetops whisper silly dreams,
In starlit nights, the moonlight beams.
Each rustling leaf a secret told,
While crickets play their songs so bold.

In the branches, laughter springs,
With sprightly tunes that nature sings.
A world of mirth, so lush and grand,
In this leafy theater, hand in hand.

Whispers of the Untamed Grove

In the woods where squirrels plot,
A raccoon juggles all he's got.
A fawn whispers to a wise old tree,
As bees team up with laughter, oh so free.

Hedgehogs roll like tiny balls,
While loons perform their silly calls.
A fox wears glasses, quite a sight,
In the glow of day, all feels just right.

The owls hoot in funky beats,
As rabbits throw their lively feats.
Grasshoppers dance in clumsy ways,
Amongst the chaos, joy always stays.

Together, they spin tales so bright,
In the forest, pure delight.
With giggles shared under the sun,
These woods are where the fun's begun.

Secrets Beneath the Canopy

Beneath the leaves, a secret spree,
Where the worms hold parties, full of glee.
A turtle raves with a funky hat,
While ants do the cha-cha, imagine that!

The mushrooms have a wiggly dance,
A ladybug twirls, given the chance.
Each root has a tale, each plant a jest,
In this green world, laughter's the best.

Squirrels invent games of tug-of-war,
While chipmunks argue, 'It's me, not you, sir!'
The groundhogs giggle, joining the fun,
As the sun smiles down, shining on everyone.

Even shadows join in, chasing about,
Echoes of laughter, never a doubt.
Beneath the trees, the secrets grow,
In this lively land, all joy will flow.

Dance of the Forest Sprites

In a clearing where the wild things twirl,
The forest sprites dance, making ears whirl.
With acorns tossed and giggles so bright,
They paint the air with pure delight.

A badger spins in polka-dot socks,
While owls wear hats made of old clocks.
Chasing the breezes, they leap through the trees,
With glee in their hearts, and laughter like bees.

Fireflies flicker, lighting the show,
As mushrooms swirl in the moon's soft glow.
The sprites wear crowns of daisies, so fine,
Whirling and twirling like leaves on the vine.

With each silly step, they share their glee,
Creating magic for all who see.
In the dance of the night, fun takes flight,
Echoing joy until morning light.

Echoes in the Thicket

In the thicket, strange sounds arise,
With each rustle, a chorus of sighs.
A porcupine punctuates the night,
With a joke so sharp, it's quite the fright.

Rabbits rehearse for a play on the spot,
While the skunks craft scents that are quite the plot.
The owls provide the music's sweet beat,
As critters tap dance with two left feet.

A hedgehog steals the show with his quill,
Telling tales that give all a thrill.
The fox tries a flip, but lands in a bush,
As laughter erupts—oh, what a rush!

Amidst the echoes that bounce and play,
The thicket's alive in the funniest way.
From whispers to chuckles, like magic in flight,
In these leafy confines, joy takes delight.

Beneath the Gnarled Branches

A squirrel juggles acorns high,
By a tree that looks like it's taking a sigh.
The leaves giggle when the wind starts to dance,
While mushrooms wear hats for a fancy romance.

The badger's on roller skates, what a sight,
Racing through shadows, oh what delight!
The owls just hoot, they don't seem to care,
As chipmunks play tag with plenty to share.

In this merry glade, hilarity grows,
With each rustle and laugh, the whole forest knows.
The rabbits tell jokes, while foxes just grin,
This woodland's a stage where nonsense can win.

So come take a peek, join the silly spree,
Beneath ancient branches, wild with glee.
Life's a banquet of laughter for each creature near,
In the embrace of the woods, fun's always here.

The Pulse of the Oakwood

Beneath the boughs of the thick, old trees,
A frog's piano plays, oh so off-key,
The beetles tap dance in a fine little line,
While butterflies twirl like they know how to shine.

The raccoons are plotting a nighttime parade,
With moonbeams as lanterns, they'll serenade.
Each critter involved, oh what a delight,
Making mischief together under starry light.

A hedgehog in glasses is reading a tome,
Claiming he'll take us all far away from home.
With riddles and giggles, he wears such a grin,
As we roll with laughter, we tumble, we spin.

So let's dance with the shadows, let hilarity ring,
With laughter and joy, the forest takes wing.
For each heartbeat of laughter beneath leafy cloak,
Is proof of the magic in these woods we stoke.

Lush Verses of the Sylva

In the lush of the bushes, oh what do we see?
An owl in a fedora sipping chamomile tea.
A snail in a shell that's all covered in bling,
Claims he's the ruler of everything.

The rabbits tell stories with a funky old twist,
Of foxes in leggings preparing for lists.
They dance on the paths, with the sun at their backs,
While critters in flannel exchange funny hacks.

The brook's giggling softly, it knows all the jokes,
While frogs in tuxedos play pranks on the folks.
And hedges are whispering secrets unseen,
About a squirrel who threw a most grand party scene.

So join in the fun, let your worries unfold,
In nature's own laughter, it's pure and it's bold.
From leafy green stages, the joy will resound,
In this merry old forest where fun can abound.

The Breath of the Forest

When morning dew glistens on each little leaf,
A bunny recites poetry, beyond belief.
With rhythm and rhyme, he hops in a way,
That makes all the foxes join in for the play.

The sun peeks through branches, what a splendid scene!
A raccoon with a flute starts a band, so keen.
While critters all gather, it's quite the event,
For in the small moments, pure silliness is spent.

The trees start to sway, a soft dance in the breeze,
As the night owls prepare to do just as they please.
With chuckles and bursts, the forest aligns,
Creating a symphony—their laughter, their signs.

So let every moment in nature remind,
Of silly adventures and joy intertwined.
With a wink and a ribbit, in shadows we trust,
The breath of the wild is both funny and just.

Treasures of the Forest Floor

A squirrel in his tiny hat,
Hides acorns 'neath the mat.
The mushrooms wear their polka dots,
Singing songs of silly thoughts.

A gnome with a grin so wide,
Beckons where the oddities hide.
Lost socks and jelly beans,
Dance with frogs in verdant scenes.

Raccoons waltz with crows in tow,
As branches swing to and fro.
A dance-off? Who'd have believed?
In this place, we're all deceived!

With trees that giggle in the breeze,
And whispers from the bumblebees.
Each treasure found ignites a cheer,
In this forest, we have no fear!

Murmurs from the Thicket

Listen close to the rustling leaves,
They share tales that no one believes.
A fox in shades of blazing red,
Tells riddles from a mushroom bed.

The thicket laughs at every turn,
As curious critters search and learn.
A rabbit with a monocle bold,
Claims he's a knight, or so I'm told.

Owls debate the best night snacks,
While hedgehogs plot their sneaky tracks.
In this wild chat, no one is bored,
The laughter echoes, never stored!

A chorus of whispers fills the air,
With secrets only the trees can share.
The thicket buzz is endless fun,
In this world, we're always young!

Realm of the Untamed

In a realm that's lush and free,
Where ants debate their next cup of tea.
A butterfly dons its finest attire,
Now that's one to inspire!

A bear who thinks he can really sing,
Carries on like a great big king.
But honey's his jam, that's for sure,
His dance moves? Utterly obscure!

The trees all cheer with branches so spry,
As lizards attempt aerial fly-bys.
Laughter's the language spoken here,
With nature's puns ringing clear.

The untamed realm is quite absurd,
With creatures chatting, not one disturbed.
Join the chorus, don't be late,
Fun in every nook awaits!

Twilight Beneath the Branches

As twilight drapes its golden cloak,
The fireflies gather, ready to poke.
A cat named Whiskers tells tall tales,
Of dragonflies with sparkly scales.

Beneath the branches, shadows prance,
As crickets and beetles lead a dance.
A hedgehog somersaults with flair,
While owls chuckle at their stare.

The moon peeks through in silver light,
A raccoon raps, it's quite a sight!
With laughter echoing all around,
In this twilight, joy is found.

So come and join this merry crowd,
Where every giggle's heartily loud.
The magic linger in the air,
Beneath the branches, let's declare!

www.ingramcontent.com/pod-product-compliance
Lightning Source LLC
Chambersburg PA
CBHW051635160426
43209CB00004B/655